THE
ACTIVATION

A 23-Day Guided Journey to Greatness

JASON SHURKA

THE ACTIVATION: A 23-DAY GUIDED JOURNEY TO GREATNESS

Library of Congress Control Number: 2025919722

Printed in the United States

PROJECT MANAGER: Crystal Edwards
INTERIOR LAYOUT AND JACKET DESIGN: Nicole Sturk

TABLE OF CONTENTS

OPENING MESSAGE

We are living in a time when more and more people are beginning to ask deeper questions. Questions like, "Why am I here?, What is my purpose?, What is truth?, and most importantly, How can I remember what I've always known deep within?".

THE ACTIVATION is not just another book filled with concepts to memorize or philosophies to adopt. It's an experiential guide meant to awaken the soul's remembrance through presence, perception, and daily meditation. Over the next 23 days, you are encouraged to read **one entry per day**, beginning tomorrow with, "Day 1: Trust the Process. Let it Flow". Each entry is designed to offer a new lens through which to see yourself and the world around you. It's simple. It's practical. And if received with an open heart, it can be life-altering.

This book doesn't aim to teach you anything new. It seeks to help you uncover what is already within you. Because the truth is, you've never been disconnected.

You've simply forgotten. And that forgetting, collectively and individually, is what this book gently guides us to transcend.

Each daily entry is written with purpose and intention. As you read each one, allow every letter to fully integrate into your awareness. The power of this book doesn't come from speed-reading it. It comes from pausing, reflecting, and aligning yourself with the energetic frequency behind each word. One idea, fully embodied, can change everything.

To support this integration process, **you will find a blank notes page following each day's message**. This is your space. Use it to write your own affirmations and intentions for the day and always do your best to ensure that your affirmations and intentions align with the messages you read daily. Before officially beginning your 23-day activation tomorrow, you will find a few blank pages following this opening message that you are encouraged to write in, with the goal of setting your intentions for the next 23 days. What is it that you would like to accomplish throughout this journey? How do you envision the most optimal version of yourself? Are you ready to commit to embodying the highest version of yourself? Today is a day of intention setting to give your activation over the next 23 days a clear direction and trajectory. This practice of translating awareness into your own words will help you ground the wisdom into your daily life and activate your inner creator. Don't overthink it. Just allow your truth to come through, in whatever form it needs to.

You may notice that this book doesn't follow a traditional format. It speaks directly to you, heart to heart, soul to soul. And as you read, you may begin to feel a resonance . . . as if the words are coming from a part of yourself that you've long forgotten but never truly lost. That's the remembrance at work. That's the awareness stirring. That's the invitation.

It's important to note: this journey is not about right or wrong, good or bad, or even what you believe. It's about direct experience. It's about feeling truth rather than debating it. Some entries may immediately click. Others may seem abstract or even challenging. That's okay. Awareness doesn't always arrive through understanding. Sometimes, it arrives through stillness and space. Trust that whatever needs to land, will.

There is no correct way to move through this book other than to be present with it. Let your intuition lead. Let your awareness guide the pace. Just commit to one entry per day, followed by a few moments of reflection, and allow each idea to shape your own unique remembrance.

This book was written to remind you of who and what you are. Not just as a body. Not just as a name or identity.

But as awareness itself—timeless, boundless, creative, and deeply connected to all that is.

This is not just information, it's an activation.
This is not just reading, it's remembering.

So, take a breath. Let go of expectations. And allow this journey to unfold.

Your awareness is your liberation.

And the journey begins now . . .

LET THE JOURNEY BEGIN . . .

*(read this to yourself, out loud, before you
write your intentions today)*

The next 23 days of my life are going to activate me in unimaginable ways. Over the next 23 days, I am going to transform every aspect of my life, past, present, and future, in the most positive way possible. All of my current limiting beliefs will become a pastime. Limitation will no longer be something that I recognize, let alone use in my vocabulary. The way that I speak will change. The way that I think will change. The way that I feel will change. The way that I respond to situations in life will change. The abundant energy that exists all around me and within me will play an active role in my daily life. Any actions leading to self-sabotage will completely dissolve for my life. The person I will become by the end of this activation will be unrecognizable in comparison to the person who I am today. I will activate any and all potential within me. I will activate the ability to think bigger without fearing what those potentials hold for me. I will activate the abundant energy all around me and within me, turning me into a magnet that attracts only the best outcomes. Through unconditional Love, unconditional forgiveness, and undoubted faith, I will reach both physical and spiritual heights that I once could never even fathom. I vow to give it my all over the next 23 days. I am absolutely dedicated to succeeding in activating every fiber of my being and my potential over the next 23 days I am here. I am capable. I am powerful. I am supported. I am blessed. I am ready. May the activation begin.

Setting My Intentions for the Activation

Use the next few pages to express your intentions, in writing, for what you wish to accomplish over the next 23 days during your activation. Once you complete this step, use the rest of the day to reflect in presence on the journey you are about to embark on. Tomorrow, you may officially begin with Day 1.

_____

_____

_____

_____

_____

_____

_____

_____

_____

_____

_____

_____

_____

_____

_____

_____

_____

_____

_____

_____

_____

_____

_____

_____

TRUST THE PROCESS.
LET IT FLOW.

Everything that happens in my life does not happen TO me, but rather FOR me. I know deep in my heart that my path is full of greatness. I know that the Divine has a plan for me that is far greater than I can ever imagine. When I let go of trying to control the outcome of every situation and simply let it flow in the way that it must, everything works out in such a way that leads to unimaginable results, far greater than my own comprehension. Whenever I try to control reaching a specific outcome, what I am actually doing is limiting the greatness that the Divine has in store for me. I have done, and will continue to do, everything in my power to bring forth the best possible outcome. I will never definitively define an outcome because doing so limits the greatness of my own path and destiny. My destiny can never be taken away from me, because it holds the truth of who I am and what I am destined to become. I may not always be able to see exactly how the process is going to unfold, and I don't have to. Why? Because I trust the process and the path ahead of me. The only thing I am in control of is how I respond to situations as they arise. From this moment onwards, I vow to see the silver lining of every situation that arises in my life. I vow to remember that everything happens FOR me, and not TO me. I vow to always take action wherever I possibly can, while always remembering that I am not the one in control of the outcome. I vow to always remember that my destiny is far greater than my own understanding. I vow to learn from every step along the way of the process unfolding. I vow to trust the process and let it flow with the ultimate faith that the unfolding process has been, and will continue to be, forever in my favor, even if I can't see how just yet. I will do my best, and let the Divine do the rest. That is my promise from this moment onwards. A promise that will forever be held deeply in my heart. I am blessed. I am abundant. I am guided. I am supported. I am Loved.

UNCONDITIONAL LOVE

Love is who I am. Love is what I am. Love is the energy that created the Universe. Love is what all of creation is based on. I recognize that sometimes, I forget to Love myself. I recognize that sometimes, I forget to Love others around me. But if Love is ever truly forgotten, what else is there? As I read these words, I feel them in my heart. I breathe the energy of Love into every fiber of my being. I find a place within my heart to Love every-thing, and every-being, especially those who I have been hurt by. Deep down, I know that those who have hurt me never intended anything personal against me. They were simply acting out of their own traumas rooted out of their own lack of Love somewhere on their own life path. To hate them will solve nothing. To Love them will heal everything. Instead of holding hate in my heart towards the individuals who have hurt me, I am now making a conscious effort to see the goodness in all beings and all things. Today, I am making a conscious effort to see how those I feel hurt by have actually helped me become a stronger and better version of myself. Today, I am making a conscious effort to channel all energies that are not in alignment with unconditional Love in a positive way. Today, I am making a conscious effort to forgive all those who I have negative feelings towards. Doing so will propel me towards my own path of greatness in a beautiful way. Today, I will make a conscious effort to visualize a cleansing energy of unconditional Love around the individuals who have hurt me in the past. I will move past all of the feelings I hold in my heart by honoring their traumas and releasing myself from the negative feelings I hold towards each and every one of them. I know that unconditional Love is the way forward. The next time I experience a negative emotion towards anybody, including myself, I will make a conscious effort to see the innocent individual doing their best to survive with their current circumstances, and I will project unconditional Love towards them. Today, I will look myself in the eyes, using a mirror, and project unconditional Love towards the incredible and miraculous reflection in front of me. I will let go of any and all judgement towards myself, regardless of my past actions. I will use the energy of unconditional Love to forge a positive path forward. I am blessed. I am abundant. I am guided. I am supported. I am Loved.

ACTIVATING ABUNDANCE

The law of conservation of energy states that energy cannot be created or destroyed. This means that energy is infinite and abundantly available throughout every fiber of the universe. Although I appear to be a physical entity, I know that everything is made up of energy, which is infinite. I am an expression of infinity and abundance. Abundance is not something I strive to attain; rather it is something that I yearn to re-member within myself. Everything that I need, I have. My health is abundant. My finances are abundant. My potential is abundant. I see through the illusion of lack and no longer align with it. From this day forward, I vow to align with the energy of abundance in all that I do. I vow to give to others from an abundant place, with the intention of keeping the abundant flow of the universe flowing. I vow to radiate the energy of abundance in all that I do and all that I am. I have undoubted faith that anything I set my mind to, I can achieve, as I know abundant potential resides within me. The mastery of life is an internal game. To win, I must dive deep within myself, where an infinite abundance of answers resides. I am abundantly healthy. I am abundantly wealthy. I am abundantly Loving. I am abundantly Loved. I am abundantly giving. I am abundantly receiving. My potential is infinite, and from this moment onwards, I vow to take action to realize that potential. I am blessed. I am abundant. I am guided. I am supported. I am Loved.

IT'S ALL GOOD

At the core of it all, all is One. Oneness does not know *this* and *that*, as it operates from the only true perspective of "is", the singularity that connects all of existence. At the core of it all, there is no "good" and "bad". Everything just "is" and all that "is" is good, with no objective opposite. Throughout all the "bad" things that occurred in my life, I have come to realize how the "bad" is truly just the greatest good in disguise. The "bad" had the highest potential of growth and evolution within it. I vow to change my relationship with the "bad" things in my life as they are truly the greatest parts of my life. I vow to find the good in absolutely everything because doing so will provide me with the ability to excel in every aspect of my life. At the core of it all, if all is One, oneness would never do anything to hurt itself, which is where my knowingness that everything is good, and only good, is rooted out of. I vow to express gratitude for the hardest situations in my life with the intention of extracting the potential of greatness from all of those ex-periences. I vow to have unconditional Love and accep-tance towards any and every experience in my life. I vow to always become conscious of and tap into the potential of any and all "bad" experiences in my life from my past, in my present, and into my future. I am blessed. I am abundant. I am guided. I am supported. I am Loved.

THE PRESENT MOMENT

The only moment that truly exists is right here, right now. What I call my past was experienced in the present moment, and what I call my future will be experienced in the present moment. I understand that sadness and regret is an expression of remaining too attached to my past, and that anxiety and nervousness is an expression of being worried about the uncertainty of my future. From this moment onwards, I vow to move on from the energy of my past and let go of the uncertainty of my future. I vow to consciously trust that process that is governed by an all-knowing power beyond my comprehension. I vow to always remember that my past is responsible for making me who I am in the present moment. I vow to always remember that my future is dictated by my present. I vow to consistently practice being right here, right now, unconditionally. Sometimes, I may succeed in doing so for just a few seconds. Other times, I may succeed in doing so for a few minutes, a few hours, or even a few days. I vow to never be attached to the length of time I can remain in a present state as that will only bring me out of the present moment. The key that I will practice throughout the day today, and the days, weeks, and years to come, is the consistent effort of experiencing the present moment, even if it's just for a few seconds at a time. The more frequently I practice accessing these short spurts of bliss, the longer these spurts will become, eventually and naturally leading me to be in a predominant state of presence in my day-to-day life. The present moment is where all creation is rooted from. It is the key to accessing my fullest potential. I vow to practice accessing this truth on a frequent basis until it becomes second nature to me. I am blessed. I am abundant. I am guided. I am supported. I am Loved.

MY BODY. MY HOME.
MY DESTINY.

My body is my sanctuary. It is the vessel that I have been given as a gift from above to experience the gift of life as a human being. My body is the foundation of all dimensions above it, and as I keep my body in the best possible shape, my potential for reaching all dimensions above it becomes possible. The cleaner I keep my body, the more capable it becomes. My body is the most advanced and unique form of technology to ever exist. It allows me to taste. It allows me to hear. It allows me to feel. It allows me to speak. It allows me to think. It allows me to dream. My body is a tool that provides me with the potential to reach unimaginable heights in this lifetime. Living in a dirty body is no different than living in a dirty home, which creates an environment for dust and mold to build up over time. Every day that I live, I have a choice to make. Do I want to live in a dirty body or do I want to live in a clean body? Up until this very moment, that choice has been an unconscious one. I am now aware of the benefits that a clean body provides me, which makes it so much easier to avoid taking actions that make me feel good temporarily, but hurt me over time. From this moment onward I vow to take care of my body. I vow to keep my body clean, while making a conscious effort to clean my body from past actions that have hurt it. I vow to do my absolute best to introduce only the best things into my body, whether it be positive affirmations, filtered water, or clean and organic food. I vow to be more conscious of how I treat my body. I vow to Love my body as it is, while making a conscious effort to move out of stagnation and move into bringing my body to its fullest potential. My body is a gift that I have received by the Divine, and I must honor and respect the frequency that I am capable of possessing within this beautiful vessel. I am grateful for the sanctuary that I call my body, and I vow to do everything in my power, from this moment onwards, to ensure that my body reaches its fullest potential with the intention of tapping into all dimensions above it. My mind. My spirit. My soul. I am blessed. I am abundant. I am guided. I am supported. I am Loved.

EMBRACING CHANGE

Change is defined as the act or instance of becoming different. Change is not my enemy. Change is my friend. I know that change can be scary because of the uncertain reality that lies before me upon making a change. I also know that change is the only way for me to become a better and more evolved version of myself. Resisting change is no different than resisting my own growth and evolution. Accepting change is the first step that must be taken in order to reach my fullest potential. Embracing change is the only way forward. There are actions that I consistently do that I know I am better off without. Many of these actions have become a part of my identity, whether spoken, or unspoken. Changing these actions can be scary because in doing so, I am changing my identity. However, I know that if I am the same person I am today in one year from now, what accomplishments have I truly achieved? Change is my friend, and therefore, it must be embraced. From today, onwards, I vow to make positive changes in my life. I vow to let go of my counterproductive actions that will ultimately lead me to a negative place. I vow to let go of the friends in my life who no longer serve my highest good. I vow to get closer to the individuals who inspire me to become the greatest version of myself. I vow to let go of any and all stagnant energy in my life. I vow to not only embrace change, but Love it in every way, shape, and form, because it is change that allows me to evolve into my greatest self. I am grateful for the ability the Divine gave me to change. I am grateful for the awareness the Divine has blessed me with allowing me to embrace change. I am grateful for the opportunity to change in the most productive ways in my life. I am blessed. I am abundant. I am guided. I am supported. I am Loved.

FORGIVENESS

Forgiveness. What is it? Forgiveness does not mean to forget. Forgiveness is the act of letting go of distorted energies and frequencies from past experiences that no longer serve me. It's not only about forgiving others, but also about forgiving myself. The act of not forgiving myself is expressed over time as regret. The act of not forgiving others is expressed over time as disease. I acknowledge that throughout my life I have been hurt by certain individuals. I acknowledge that I still hold some of that pain within myself today. I acknowledge that I've made mistakes in my past. I acknowledge that I am still holding onto the pain of some of these mistakes instead of seeing them as opportunities to learn and to grow from, which would ultimately lead me to a point of complete energetic flow throughout my entire being. Having compassion for myself and others is the first and most important step that must be taken to truly forgive. It is through the energy of compassion that forgiveness arises because compassion allows me to understand and remember that everybody is simply doing their best given their life circumstances at the time. The energy of forgiveness brings forth the reality of healing and remembering my wholeness. Today, I vow to forgive myself of all past mistakes through reshaping my relationship with these mistakes by understanding that they are all opportunities for me to learn and to further evolve. I vow to forgive all those who have hurt me in the past by remembering that it was never personal, although their actions may have felt personal. I vow to bring forth the energy of forgiveness into my life in every way possible. I vow to be less hard on myself because I know that doing so will truly bring me nowhere in the long run. I vow to embody one of the fundamental traits of the Divine, unconditional forgiveness for all, in honor of unity, wellness, and Love. I am blessed. I am abundant. I am guided. I am supported. I am Loved.

THE POWER OF BOUNDARIES

What is a boundary? A boundary is a productive limitation that I set for both myself, and for others, in order to keep me on track with the intention of honoring my highest path and my highest potential. I acknowledge that sometimes, due to a lack of boundaries set with myself, I put myself in positions that lead to undesirable outcomes. I acknowledge that due to a lack of boundaries set with others, I put myself into undesirable positions. Setting boundaries is the key to continue growing and evolving into the most empowered version of myself. The word "yes" can lead to both incredible and horrible places. Saying "yes" to counterproductive actions out of the satisfaction of experiencing instant gratification will only lead to undesirable destinations in the long run. Saying "yes" out of the fear of upsetting another individual will always lead to an undesirable outcome for both myself, and that individual. I must always remember that the key is not to please others in the short run in exchange for sacrificing myself and what genuinely excites me because without excitement and inspiration, I will let that individual down anyway. I must remember that saying "no" is not a bad thing if it is coming from a place of honoring my true authentic will. Setting boundaries with both myself, and with others, from an authentic place, is the key to liberation, true happiness, and reaching my fullest potential. Today, I vow to make a conscious effort to identify where productive boundaries are not yet set and take aligned action right away. I vow to honor myself and my true authentic will. I vow to distance myself from any actions rooted out of the desire of experiencing instant gratification. Anything connected to instant gratification is a clear indication that although I may be satisfied in the short term, such an action will lead to undesirable outcomes in the long run. Healthy boundaries are my friend, and I intend to begin setting more of them beginning right here, right now. I am blessed. I am abundant. I am guided. I am supported. I am Loved.

_____

_____

_____

_____

_____

_____

_____

_____

_____

_____

_____

_____

_____

_____

_____

_____

_____

_____

_____

_____

_____

_____

_____

_____

_____

_____

STEPPING INTO FLOW

Flow is what I am. Flow is who I am. Flow is what allows my heart to consistently beat. Flow is what allows my blood to consistently flow. Flow is the fundamental essence of the universe. Flow is not an act of doing, rather an act of being. Sometimes, I get in my own way and interrupt the effortless flow of energy within me. The disruption of this flow leads to confusion, disappointment, and a lack of creativity, among many other undesirable feelings and emotions. In order to consistently remain in flow, I must make a conscious effort to embody the energy of undoubted faith, which is a major key to access effortless flow. The liberating truth is that flow arises out of simply being present and focusing on what is directly in front of me. I acknowledge that throughout my life, there have been many moments where I have disrupted my own internal and external effortless flow as a result of lacking trust and faith in the Divine. Today, I vow to make a conscious effort to focus on my state of being with the intention of being present and in flow. Today, just like every day, circumstances will arise that may make it easy for me to fall out of my effortless flow if I'm only focused on my state of doing, as opposed to my state of being. As these circumstances arise, I will continuously remind myself that flow is an effortless energy because of the fact that it is the fundamental essence of the universe. I vow to always remember that there is a Divine plan at play, greater than my own comprehension, and through undoubted faith, everything will work out and unfold perfectly if I simply just allow everything to be as it is. I vow to radiate this awareness and knowingness everywhere I go, and to whoever is around me, with the intention of bringing forth this reality to not only the world within me, but to the world around me as well. I am blessed. I am abundant. I am guided. I am supported. I am Loved.

CONSCIOUS COMMUNICATION

The art of conscious communication, when mastered, leads to very high places. What is the difference between communication and conscious communication? Well, communication is simply sharing your thoughts and perspectives through the expression of words to another individual or a group of individuals. The issue is that sometimes, misunderstandings and misinterpretations occur, leading to divisive realities. This is where conscious communication plays a pivotal role. Conscious communication includes gauging an individual with the intention of becoming aware of the level of understanding and awareness that individual possesses within themselves. Conscious communication is the art of meeting others where they are at as opposed to just speaking to others from where I am at. Conscious communication always leads to a more productive and united form of conversation. To achieve this, I must make a conscious effort to put myself in the shoes of the individual or individuals I am communicating with. To do this, I must have compassion for their thoughts and their beliefs, even if I don't agree with them. Doing so will allow others, and especially those who hold different beliefs than I do, to feel a more familiar, friendly, and comfortable dynamic energy when communicating with me, as opposed to feeling attacked and taking on a defense. In honor of more productive relationships and communication in my life and the life of everyone I interact with, I vow to practice conscious communication on a daily basis. I promise to make a conscious effort to understand the perspectives of those I am communicating with, even if I don't agree with them. I vow to accept everyone who I interact with as they are, regardless of their thoughts and beliefs. I vow to give space for all perspectives and never take on a defense if somebody opposes my personal opinions, thoughts, and beliefs. This is the art of conscious communication, and today, I will make a conscious effort to begin mastering it. I am blessed. I am abundant. I am guided. I am supported. I am Loved.

EMBRACE ACCEPTANCE.
DISSOLVE RESISTANCE.

Acceptance is a beautiful skill to master. Its opposite, known as resistance, is what brings upon all negative experiences in my life. 10% of life is what happens to me. 90% of life is how I choose to respond to it. In other words, the way that I choose to respond to a situation has to potential to change the entire situation. When I resist what is, I create an environment of energetic blockages, only making the situation worse. When I simply accept what is, I create an environment of energetic flow, which is when the next best course of action arises immediately. Choosing to accept what is with no judgment towards a situation is the first step that I must always take in order to change that situation into a more desirable one. What I resist, persists, which is why resisting what is will only create more of that very thing. In honor of aligning with my highest path and tapping into my highest potential, I vow to take the first and most important step today which is accepting all that is, in the way that it is, all with the intention of gaining clarity on the next best course of action to take in order to align with my highest good and my greatest potential. I vow to always remember that my quality of life is not dictated by what happens to me but rather how I respond to those experiences. My response, alone, is what dictates my relationship to any and every circumstance and experience that arises in my life. Acceptance of all that is with no judgment is the key to generating a productive response. I accept all that is. I hold gratitude in my heart for every one of my life circumstances and experiences, especially the difficult ones, because it is within those experiences that exist the seeds of my greatest potential. Resistance no longer has a place in my life. Acceptance is the only way forward. I am blessed. I am abundant. I am guided. I am supported. I am Loved.

THE POWER OF FOCUS

Energy goes where attention flows. My ability to focus my attention on something specific is the most powerful tool I possess. Focus is my superpower. Focus gives me the ability to create whatever I desire, whenever I desire. Ultimately, what I focus on is what I manifest. I acknowledge that sometimes, I unintentionally focus on what I don't want, which is rooted out of emotions such as worry and anxiety. Although these counterproductive emotions are rooted out of a place of wanting the best for myself, I am aware that these counterproductive emotions and actions only lead to undesirable outcomes. While intention can enhance the way I use my superpower of focus, intention without aligned focus will not bring me very far. For example, "I don't want to be sick" holds the intention of wanting to be healthy; however, my focus in this case is on sickness, which is misaligned and will only create a reality in which I continue to experience sickness. On the other hand, "Thank you for giving me the ability to be healthy" is a direct reflection of both aligned intention and aligned focus. It is imperative that I use my ability to focus on something specific in a productive and aligned way. Thoughts and words are made up of frequencies, and it is those frequencies that make up the reality that I experience. Through shifting my focus in a conscious and aligned way, I am able to manipulate the frequencies that make up my reality, through aligned thought and speech, leading to a desirable reality. Today, I vow to make myself aware of the subjects that I focus on throughout the day, both spoken and unspoken. Today, I vow to focus specifically on the realities I genuinely want to experience. Today, I will use my power of visualization to see myself in my desired reality. Today, I will live as if I am already experiencing my desired reality. I am blessed. I am abundant. I am guided. I am supported. I am Loved.

IMPOSSIBLE IS IMPOSSIBLE

The only thing that is impossible is impossibility itself. The fact is, energy cannot be created or destroyed. This means that energy is infinite. Reality is made up of energy. This means that reality must also be infinite. Limitation cannot exist in infinity. I, too, am made up of energy. Since energy is infinite, and I am made up of energy, I must also be infinite. Fundamentally, there is no such as impossible. Any and all limitations that I experience in my life are a result of my own belief system. At some point throughout my childhood, I believed that impossibility was true because those who I Love and respect and those who raised me told me so. Today is the day that everything changes. Today is the day I recognize that although those individuals meant well, they still imposed their limiting beliefs on me, which I accepted because I didn't know any better at the time. Today, I know better. Today, I am more aware. Today, I am more knowledgeable. Today, I break through all barriers, including the illusion of impossibility. The fact is, everything is possible. I am the one who makes that true. It is possible for me to live an abundant life, a healthy life, a joyous life, a life full of Love, a life full of laughter, a family-oriented life, a life full of friends, and a life full of gratitude. It is already happening as a potential of the infinite realities that exist right here, right now. Impossibility is an illusion. Possibility is the only thing that truly exists. I am blessed. I am abundant. I am guided. I am supported. I am Loved.

MY VIBRATION IS MY REALITY

The law of vibration states that I experience what I am in resonance with. In other words, the reality that I experience is a direct reflection of the vibration that I hold. This means that I am responsible for everything that I have ever experienced in the past and will ever experience in the future. My life is a reflection of my thoughts, my beliefs, and my words, which are all made up of different frequencies. As I radiate these frequencies, I resonate with realities of those same frequencies and, therefore, experience those realities. It's no different than how a radio functions. Factually speaking, each radio station is hosted on a different frequency. Through the usage of the tuner, I can choose which station I want to listen to whether it is rap, country, opera, and so on. My thoughts, my beliefs, and my words, are my tuner. They are the tools that allow me to tune into one reality over another. Up until now, I may have not been aware of this fact. I may have used my thoughts, my beliefs, and my words, in an unconscious way leading to the undesirable experiences that I am experiencing in my life today. The liberating truth is that I have the power to change this at any present moment. By simply choosing to focus on my speech, which is ultimately a reflection of my thoughts, and my beliefs, I can change my reality. Through repetitive speech, I have the power to imprint my own thoughts and beliefs until they are forced to match the frequency of my speech. Writing in a repetitive manner to reflect my conscious and repetitive speech can only enhance my ability to positively imprint my thoughts and my beliefs. Repetition is key. These are the tools that I have at my fingertips to change my vibration in a conscious way, and therefore to change my reality. Today, I will pay more attention to my thoughts, my beliefs, and my words. Today, I will use repetitive speech in a conscious way to positively and productively impact and imprint my thoughts and beliefs. Today, I will use my ability to write in such a way that reflects my conscious and repetitive speech with the intention of further enhancing my power to imprint my thoughts and beliefs. Today, I consciously take responsibility for all realities that I've tuned into thus far throughout my life in an unconscious way. I look forward to now consciously tuning into my desired realities through my newfound awareness of the law of vibration and its application. I am blessed. I am abundant. I am guided. I am supported. I am Loved.

THE SECRET OF CONSISTENT PROGRESS

Progress is something that I strive for in every aspect of my life. I always aim to continue evolving and becoming a better version of myself. I acknowledge that sometimes when I say I will do something, like a New Year's resolution, I start off strong but eventually, my motivation and discipline fade away, leading to a lack of consistency and a lack of progress. I've come to understand that I lose traction when the milestones I set for myself are too far away from one another. The secret of consistent progress is not ambitious goals that require an extraordinary amount of discipline to achieve, but rather by creating a system to achieve small wins along the way to my desired destination. The power of small wins must never be underestimated. Naturally, I am more inclined to do something when I am good at it because being good at something is satisfying to me. By simply setting smaller milestones that are more easily reachable along my path, I will experience small and satisfying wins along the way that give me the natural motivation to want to keep moving forward. Although I have very big goals and aspirations, I must acknowledge who I am and how I operate as a human being. Winning is satisfying to me. Reaching a milestone gives me more motivation so I no longer have to depend on discipline that naturally fades away over time. Today, I will identify my greatest goals and aspirations. Today, I will create a system made up of more reachable milestones along the way to ultimately reach my goals and aspirations. Today, I will celebrate any and all small wins along the way and I will use the satisfaction of each win as the fuel to experiencing consistent progress throughout my life. I am a winner. I look forward to reaching my greatest goals and aspirations through the power of small wins. I am blessed. I am abundant. I am guided. I am supported. I am Loved.

ACCESSING INFINITE CREATIVITY

Creativity is an expression of the infinite Divine intelligence of the Universe. To access creativity in an effortless way, I must come into resonance with this infinite Divine intelligence, which makes up the Universe and all of creation as we know it, both seen and unseen. Creativity is not a state of doing. Creativity is a state of being. To tap into the creative genius that exists within me, presence is key. Creativity and the effortless flow of creation are synonymous. Since I am one with effortless energetic flow, Divine and infinite creative genius is inherent with me. Instead of attempting to DO something creative with the intention of accessing creativity, I must simply act as a vessel to invite and allow Divine, infinite, and effortless creative intelligence to flow through me. The truth is, I am already doing this in every given moment. My heart is constantly tapped into Divine and effortless creation as expressed through its own beat.

My blood is constantly tapped into Divine and effortless creation as expressed through its own flow. My cells are constantly tapped into Divine and effortless creation as expressed through their own replication. Instead of trying to be creative through the act of doing, I must always remember that I am already tapped into Divine and infinite creativity through the act of simply BEING. I am a Divine creator. I am always tapped into the infinite intelligence of creation. Being present is the key to tapping into my own creative power. I am a vessel that Divine, intelligent, and effortless creation flows through. I am capable of absolutely anything. Today, I vow to be present with the intention of tapping into effortless creativity. Today, I vow to invite a higher degree of creativity into my life. Today, I will succeed in tapping into the inherent and innate Divine creative intelligence that resides within me. I am blessed. I am abundant. I am guided. I am supported. I am Loved.

DAY 18

THE ENERGY OF GRATITUDE

Gratitude is a beautiful energy that brings forth the best of all realities. There is a fine line between gratitude and pride. Pride implies that I am the source of greatness, an emotion rooted out of the consciousness of separation. Gratitude implies that I am simply a vessel allowing for greatness to flow through, an emotion rooted out of the consciousness of unity and wellness. Gratitude brings forth coherency which always leads to an abundance of health, wealth, and happiness. Expressing gratitude gives me the ability and opportunity to resonate and align with positive and productive realities. Gratitude gives me the ability to focus on what I do have as opposed to focusing on what I perceive that I lack. Focusing on what I do have creates more of that reality. Expressing gratitude for the harder circumstances that I am dealing with in my life today provides me with the ability to change my relationship with these life circumstances and find the silver lining with each and every one of them. Today, I will consciously express gratitude for all of my blessings and all that I have been given. Today, I will express gratitude for all the things in my life that I usually don't pay attention to and take for granted, like the ability to breathe, the ability to walk, the ability to speak, the ability to think, and the ability to function in the way that I am capable of. Today, I vow to express gratitude for all aspects and levels of creation all the way from the atom in the microcosm to the galaxies in the macrocosm. Gratitude is my greatest tool and resource to create coherency and balance in all aspects of my life. Today, I vow to see the miracle and blessings of existence as a whole. I am grateful to have been given the ability to express gratitude for all of creation. I am blessed. I am abundant. I am guided. I am supported. I am Loved.

THE BEAUTY OF FAILURE

It's time to reshape my relationship with failure. Since the beginning of time, failure has been perceived as something negative. However, the greatest accomplishments in life were only achieved through repetitive failed attempts that eventually lead to success. This means that failure is actually not something negative, rather a necessary and positive step along the path to success. Failure provides me with the opportunity to learn in order to bring myself one step closer to success. Failure is not my enemy. Failure is my friend. Today, I vow to identify the failures that have brought me to what I have accomplished up until this very day. With this newfound awareness, I will perceive my failures moving forward as the very steps that bring me closer to success. Today, I vow to appreciate and express gratitude for my failures because within every failure exists a profound seed of success. Through reshaping and redefining my relationship with failure, I am able to channel the energy behind every failure moving forward into a reality of success. I am blessed. I am abundant. I am guided. I am supported. I am Loved.

FINANCIAL ABUNDANCE

For many, financial abundance is perceived to be a difficult reality to attain. The truth is, money is simply a physical expression and tool that represents energy. Reshaping my relationship with money is synonymous with reshaping my relationship with energy. The difference between $1 and $10 is a zero. The difference between $10 and $100 is a 0. The difference between $100 and $1,000 is a 0. The difference between $1000 and $10,000 is 0. The difference between $10,000 and $100,000 is a 0. The difference between $100,000 and $1,000,000 is 0. If I can generate $1,000 then I can generate $100,000 by applying the same method and mechanism once I remove my limiting beliefs around money. If I can generate $1,000,000 then I can generate $100,000,000 by applying the same method and mechanism once I remove my limiting beliefs around money. The idea that it is difficult to attain financial wealth is a limiting belief that is fundamentally not true. However, by possessing such a limiting belief, I resonate with a reality of lack and therefore begin to perpetuate a cyclical reality of lack. I must always remember that money is simply a physical expression of energy. The simplest and easiest way to generate financial abundance is not by focusing on making more money, rather focusing on how to create more value for others. The more value I create, the more value I receive. I am aware of the fact that life is one big game of energy. To master the game, I must master the laws of energy, frequency, and vibration. I am already living a life of abundance; however, sometimes I forget this fundamental truth. The effortless beat of my heart is proof that I am already tapped into an abundant source of energy. The effortless flow of my blood along with every inhale I take and every exhale I make is proof of this abundant source of energy as well. I don't have to find this abundance outside of me because I am a living testimony that it already exists within me. By simply remembering that fact and bringing forth that awareness and knowingness to my state of financial abundance, achieving and attracting financial wealth becomes effortless. I am a generator of abundant energy, therefore, giving me the ability to be a receiver of abundant energy as well. Today, I vow to remind myself that the difference between $1 and $1,000,000 is just a few zeros. Today, I vow to remind myself that the difficulty of attaining just a few more 0's is a false and limiting belief that no longer exists in my current reality. Today, I vow to bring forth undoubted faith towards the ability to align and resonate with an abundant reality in all ways. This undoubted faith provides me the ability to not be caught up on the details of how things will unfold because through this undoubted faith, I simply know in every fiber of my being that this reality will unfold in a perfect manner. I am blessed. I am abundant. I am guided. I am supported. I am Loved.

CONSCIOUS CONSUMPTION

The food that I eat is more than just food. It is a physical expression of the sustenance that my body needs to operate and function in an optimal way. Over the past few decades, humanity has become less and less connected to their food. We're now at a point where we call certain things "food" that could not be further from what food truly and naturally is. The food that I consume holds a specific frequency and energy, whereas that energy actually becomes a part of me through the absorption of matter during the digestion process. When I consume energetically distorted food, I inherit energetic distortion in my body leading to physical, emotional, and spiritual imbalances and diseases. When I consume energetically coherent food, I inherit energetic distortion in my body, leading to physical, emotional, and spiritual balance and health. The food I consume is a tool and resource that I can use to create a better overall vibration of being for myself, thus allowing me to align with optimal and desired realities. The food I consume also consist of water that has a molecular structure which is dictated by the energies and frequencies imprinted upon that water. It has been scientifically proven that when I bless my water with positive affirmations and positive intention, the molecular structure of that water takes on a more coherent shape. The opposite is true as well. When I do not bless my water and express negative affirmations and intentions towards it, the molecular structure of the water within my food takes on a distorted shape. The shape of the molecular structures on the water I consume has a direct correlation to the energy I am inheriting. In essence, when I bless my food before consuming it, I will inherit coherent energetic fields from the water in my food, leading to balance and health within my body. Now that I am aware of this fact, I vow to make a habit out of blessing any and all food that I consume with the intention of restructuring the molecular formations of the water within the food for a more positive outcome for myself. Today, I vow to be more conscious of the quality of food I choose to consume as it has a direct correlation to the quality of life that I live. I am grateful for the ability to be able to eat in the first place. I am grateful for all food, water, and the qualities that both allow me to inherit in order to live a higher quality of life. I am blessed. I am abundant. I am guided. I am supported. I am Loved.

ONENESS

All is One and One is all. For millennia, humanity has believed in the illusion of separation. Living according to this false reality has resulted in disease, war, crime, and so many more undesirable realities. The truth is, everything is connected to everything. To take it a step even further, nothing exists outside of me but rather is a result of the One consciousness that I am connected to. Just as my body is One organism made up of trillions of individual pieces, the Universe is no different. The macrocosm is a reflection of the microcosm. The microcosm is a reflection of the macrocosm. Both are infinite, and both are part of the same whole. Today, I vow to see the beauty in all of creation, regardless of its expression. Today, I vow to see and feel the interconnectedness of absolutely everything, seen and unseen, in the infinite universe. Today, I vow to tap into this Universal Awareness with the intention of seeing it spread like an infinite wildfire all around me and within me. Today,

I vow to treat every thing and every being as if it were myself because ultimately all things and all beings, including myself, are a spark of the all and simply hold a different perspective of the One and Ultimate Divine Light. I am blessed. I am abundant. I am guided. I am supported. I am Loved.

APPRECIATING DIFFICULTY

I, like everyone else, experience difficult situations in my life. Since the beginning of time, difficult situations have been deemed undesirable for obvious reasons. What would my life be like without difficult situations and experiences that arise? It would be colorless, boring, and not worth living. I acknowledge that it is the difficult situations and experiences in my life that have made me the individual who I am today. I acknowledge that it is the difficult situations and experiences in my life that give me the ability to grow and evolve. Without difficulty, there would be no growth. Without growth, there would be no purpose to life. It's time for me to redefine my relationship with difficult situations and experiences. I've experienced both low points and high points in my life. Up until today, I've considered the low points as "bad" and the high points as "good". Today, I recognize that this perception is false. It's time for me to remember that the low points in my life are where I receive new tools to evolve further and the high points in my life are where I apply the tools that I received throughout my low points. Therefore, the difficult situations in life give me tools to grow, while the easier situations in life are the very proof that I mastered the tools that I received prior. What would my life be like if I were given a new tool, I mastered it, and that's where it all ended? It would be a life with no adventure, no growth, and no evolution. A life that I would never want to live. The difficult situations and experiences in my life are opportunities and gifts given to me by the Divine. They are here to help me, not hurt me. With this newfound awareness, although difficult situations in my future may still be hard for me to cope with, I can now be grateful when they arise because I now know their true purpose in my heart and my soul. A good purpose. I am grateful for all of my past difficult experiences as they have made me who I am today and I look forward to all of my future difficult experiences because each and every one of them hold the potential for a greater version of my current self that will ultimately be realized as I master the lessons behind each of these difficult situations and experiences. I am blessed. I am abundant. I am guided. I am supported. I am Loved.

THE RETURN TO REMEMBRANCE

If you've made it to this page, then it's clear, you didn't just read this book. You journeyed through it. And that's a completely different thing because *THE ACTIVATION* was never meant to be "read." It was meant to be *remembered*. One day at a time. One layer at a time. One veil lifted, one truth revealed, one breath deepened.

Now, here we are . . . 23 days later.

So much can change in 23 days when we simply allow awareness to do what awareness does best, illuminate and activate. It doesn't force. It doesn't rush. It simply reveals. And once something is revealed, it can never be unseen again. That's the beauty of awareness—it expands in one direction only. Forward.

If you feel different right now, it's because you are. If you see the world differently now, it's because you've expanded your lens. If your inner world feels lighter, clearer, or more grounded, it's because the truth you've remembered throughout these pages was *already within you*; this book just mirrored it back to you in a way you were ready to receive.

Let's be clear: this isn't the end. In fact, this is just the beginning. Because activation is not a destination. It's a *way of being*. It's not a badge you earn. It's a frequency you embody.

WHAT NOW?

You might be asking, "What do I do next?"

The answer: *live it.* Integrate it. Breathe it. Share it. Not by preaching, but by *being*. Because the world doesn't need more teachers, it needs more examples. More embodiment. More resonance. The way you choose to show up now, in the small moments and the big ones, has a ripple effect far beyond what you can see.

You've been given tools. You've cultivated insights. You've written your own affirmations, intentions, reflections, and realizations. You've activated parts of yourself that may have been dormant for years, maybe even lifetimes. Now it's time to bring all of that into motion, and most importantly, keep it in motion.

Remember: you don't need to *know* the entire path to walk it. Just take one conscious step . . . and then another.

Let your awareness guide your choices.
Let your presence shape your relationships.
Let your breath ground you back into now.
Let your *being* speak louder than your words ever could.

And when life gets noisy, as it inevitably does, come back here. Not just to the pages of this book, but to the still space *within* you that this book helped you remember. That place is always accessible. It was never lost. It was simply waiting for you to pause long enough to *notice*.

THE SHIFT IS HAPPENING

We are living through a time of rapid transformation, individually and collectively. More people than ever before are waking up from the illusion, questioning the narrative, and feeling the pull to return to something ancient, simple, and real.

What you do with your awareness now isn't just about you. Your frequency affects the collective. Your peace ripples outward.
Every time you dissolve fear, you dissolve it for the whole.
Every time you embody Love, you strengthen it for all.
Every time you choose truth, you make it safer for others to do the same.

Never underestimate the power of one fully present, fully aware human being. That one . . . becomes a lighthouse.

So, if you've been asking, "What's my role in all this?"
The answer is simple: *hold the light.*
Live in alignment. Speak with integrity. Walk with humility. And lead with Love.
That's it. That's enough. That's everything.

YOU ARE THE REMINDER

You may not realize this yet, but by walking this path . . . *you've become the message.*

You don't have to push this awareness on others. You don't have to prove anything to anyone. All you must do is *be the example that others can feel.*

When people feel your presence, they'll remember something ancient within themselves.

You'll become a walking mirror. A frequency tuner. A quiet invitation to remember.

And you'll begin to see the magic unfold in the most subtle ways:

Someone opens up to you in a way they never have before.

A "coincidence" leads you exactly where you need to go.
A solution shows up the moment you surrender to the problem.
Your body begins to speak more clearly.
Your heart begins to lead more confidently.
And your soul . . . it begins to shine through the cracks that used to be walls.

That's when you know the awareness is *embodied*.
That's when you know the remembering is *real*.

CLOSING MESSAGE

You don't need to rush.
You don't need to force.
You don't need to chase some abstract spiritual perfection.

You're already enough.
You're already whole.
You've always been.

And now, you're aware of it.

Keep nurturing your awareness.
Keep coming back to the breath.
Keep asking new questions.
Keep unlearning what doesn't feel true.
Keep walking gently, fiercely, and with purpose.

This is your time.
This is our time.
And the world is ready.

May your life now reflect the light you've remembered.
May your words carry the vibration of your truth.
May your actions ripple through this world in the name
of Love, Balance, Unity, and Freedom.

Thank you for walking this journey.
Thank you for remembering who you are.
Thank you for choosing ACTIVATE YOUR HIGHEST
POTENTIAL.

The path is open.
The Light is on.
And your next step . . . is waiting.

Enjoy . . . THE ACTIVATION.

With Infinite Love & Blessings,
Jason Yosef Shurka

ABOUT THE AUTHOR

Jason Shurka is an author, producer and spiritual teacher who has dedicated his life to sharing spiritual truths with humanity as a whole all with the intention of waking up the human collective to its true power within. Jason has written four books and produced world-renowned movies. He is also the founder of both UNIFYD TV and UNIFYD Healing. Learn more about Jason at Jasonshurka.com.